BLACK HEROES

BLACK HEROES

51 Inspiring People from Ancient Africa to Modern-Day U.S.A.

A BLACK HISTORY BOOK FOR KIDS

ARLISHA NORWOOD, PhD

ILLUSTRATIONS BY
ANASTASIA MAGLOIRE WILLIAMS

ROCKRIDGE
PRESS

Interior and Cover Designer: Brian Lewis
Art Producer: Michael Hardgrove
Editor: Mary Colgan

Illustration © 2020 Anastasia Magloire Williams

Author photos courtesy of © Lemark Photography

ISBN: Print 978-1-64152-704-0 | eBook 978-1-64152-705-7

R1

To my past, present, and future heroes

CONTENTS

INTRODUCTION

You are a musician who wows audiences with a new sound. You are an Olympic track star who breaks records and wins several gold medals. You are an African pharaoh or queen who builds modern marvels that will capture the world's attention forever. Welcome to a world of heroes and inspirational figures. Beyond these pages you will learn about extraordinary figures from the past and present. Many of them encountered obstacles and adversity, but persevered to make history. I invite you to learn their triumphs and trials. Absorb their strength. Grasp their courage. Glide graciously through time and space and take in sights from ancient Africa to the White House. Although their feats may seem impossible, I ask you to not only learn but to imagine yourself as Duke Ellington, Jesse Owens, King Tut, and Nefertiti. The heroes that you'll learn about are from many different paths and backgrounds, but they are united by one goal: to transform the world. It is my hope that while you are reading, you imagine the endless paths to find your passion and make an impact. Lastly, I offer you these accounts as an introduction. There are more heroes to learn about. Go beyond these pages. Let the stories move you to explore other fascinating change agents that will inspire you beyond your wildest dreams.

HATSHEPSUT

c. 1507–1458 BCE

Hatshepsut was an ancient Egyptian ruler and was the longest-ruling and most successful female pharaoh.

Hatshepsut was born into royalty around 1507 BCE. Her father and her brothers were both pharaohs, which made her a princess. But she became a powerful ruler in her own right—perhaps the most powerful female pharaoh in all of Egyptian history.

Hatshepsut's reign began in 1478 BCE when she married Pharaoh Thutmose II at age 12. When her husband died, she ruled in place of his son, who was only an infant. At some point, however, Hatshepsut proclaimed herself pharaoh rather than continuing to act as the boy's regent until he was old enough to rule. Many Egyptians referred to Hatshepsut as a king, not a queen, because she ordered that paintings and sculptures depict her that way.

As a ruler, Hatshepsut worked with neighboring kingdoms to create relationships, and she opened new trade routes. She sent out several expeditions to foreign lands that brought back valuable goods like gold, furs, and incense. Though history suggests she was cunning and could be ruthless, Egypt was a wealthy and peaceful place during her rule.

Hatshepsut also dedicated her reign to building magnificent temples and monuments, which were important because they ensured work for those who were less fortunate. Her most impressive building was her mortuary temple, which is located in the Valley of the Kings, a burial place for all of Egypt's most powerful pharaohs. This grand temple became the standard for all future pharaohs. Many of Hatshepsut's buildings are now recognized as architectural marvels.

Hatshepsut died at a young age, and many believe she was poisoned. Following her death, pharaohs attempted to erase her from Egyptian history, possibly to hide the fact that a woman had been pharaoh. And they were almost successful. Her reign was unknown to scholars for many centuries until researchers began to dig deeper into ancient texts, which pointed to a powerful woman ruler. Today, you can find Hatshepsut's artifacts in nearly every major museum.

> "Queens, especially the great ones like Nefertiti and Cleopatra, capture our imaginations. But it is perhaps Hatshepsut, who was both king and queen, who is the most fascinating."

—Dr. Zahi Hawass, speaking of the discovery of Hatshepsut's mummy

EXPLORE MORE!

To learn more about Hatshepsut and other African queens, check out *Queen Like Me: The True Story of Girls Who Changed the World* by Dr. Kimberly Brown Pellum.

NEFERTITI

c. 1370–1330 BCE

Nefertiti was a famous Egyptian queen. She was known throughout the kingdom for her unmatched beauty and wisdom.

Nefertiti, also known as Neferneferuaten-Nefertiti, was likely born around 1370 BCE, but little else is known about her birth and childhood. However, many scholars believe she was born into a royal family. When she was 15, she married the pharaoh Amenhotep IV, who later changed his name to Akhenaten. Together they had six daughters.

Nefertiti ruled as queen at her husband's side. Though it isn't proven, images found in royal tombs suggest she may have had equal power with him. She is shown in dominant positions, such as acting as a priest and even striking enemies. Whether or not it is true that she was her husband's co-ruler, the artifacts show that she was respected. There are as many images of her as of her husband in artworks and historical writings. In one drawing, she and her husband are shown sitting in thrones that are the same size. They are also shown embracing in some artwork, which suggests they had an affectionate relationship.

Nefertiti's time as queen led to many changes in Egypt. When Nefertiti was in power, Egyptians worshipped several gods. Nefertiti and Akhenaten created a new religious practice, calling on all Egyptians to pray to only one god, named Aten. Their devotion to their god is clear in their names, as they both chose names that included the word *aten*.

Curiously, Nefertiti's presence later disappears from Egyptian history. She is not shown in any artwork after 1343 BCE. Although some scholars believe she may have simply passed away, others have suggested that Nefertiti became a pharaoh herself. Like other powerful women in Egypt, it's possible that she took another name and ruled the kingdom after her husband's death.

In 1912, a bust of Nefertiti was discovered in an archaeological dig in Egypt. (A bust is a sculpture of a person's head and shoulders.) The bust of Nefertiti was in surprisingly good condition considering how long it lay hidden under rubble. Many people wanted this remarkable artifact because its lifelike depiction offered a new glimpse into Nefertiti's life and resounding beauty. It reignited the public's interest in ancient Egypt. Today, the bust remains on display in Berlin, Germany.

> "Beautiful are the beauties of Aten, a beautiful woman has come."
>
> —Meaning of the name Nefertiti, which she likely chose for herself

EXPLORE MORE!

See photographs and read more about the bust of Nefertiti by searching on ancient-egypt-online.com.

TUTANKHAMUN (KING TUT)

c. 1342–1325 BCE

Tutankhamun, known as King Tut, was likely the youngest pharaoh in Egypt. He became known worldwide when his magnificent tomb was discovered.

Little is known about King Tut's early childhood. He grew up in a royal family and took the throne as king before the age of 10. Because of this, he is known as "the boy king."

The pharaoh before Tut, Akhenaten (who ruled with Nefertiti), was likely Tut's father. Egypt was in turmoil when the boy king came into power. As he was so young, Tut's advisers likely held most of the power during his rulership. With their help, he restored Egypt to its former glory by rebuilding temples and other holy sites. He also brought back the traditional worship of many gods that Akhenaten had undone and moved the people back to the old royal city, which Akhenaten had abandoned.

Unfortunately, King Tut passed away at a young age, when he was only 18 or 19. He was unknown to history until his extravagant tomb was discovered by archaeologists in 1922. When they entered the first chamber, they were astonished by what they found. The walls were painted with murals that told the life story of King Tut, his funeral, and his passage to the afterlife. The tomb included artifacts and relics such as precious jewelry and statues made from gold and ebony. The tomb was made up of four rooms, each containing thousands of priceless relics.

King Tut's coffin and corpse were well preserved, giving scientists a rare look into the lives of ancient Egyptians. The most extraordinary thing they found was the elaborate gold mask that covered King Tut's face. Today, the mask is considered one of the most famous works of art from ancient Egypt. Though he was not an especially powerful ruler, the discovery of King Tut's tomb made him an important figure in our understanding of ancient Egypt. Many of the treasures found with him have been displayed in the world's most important museums.

"[A]s my eyes grew accustomed to the light, details of the room within emerged slowly from the mist, strange animals, statues, and gold— everywhere the glint of gold."

—Howard Carter,
speaking of the discovery of King Tut's tomb

EXPLORE MORE!

You can find photos of the diary of Howard Carter online to read his first-person account of finding King Tut's tomb.

MANSA MUSA

c. 1280–1337

Mansa Musa was a prominent and wealthy ruler of Mali, a vast empire that once covered much of western Africa.

Mansa Musa was raised in a wealthy family of rulers. Research suggests he was directly related to a founder of the Mali Empire. Musa rose to power when the king went on a journey to explore the Atlantic Ocean and left Musa in charge. The king never returned. Musa became the ruler and was given the title "Mansa," which means "emperor."

Mansa Musa increased the size of the empire by claiming victory over several other kingdoms, including the city of Timbuktu, which was already an important trading post. One of the world's first universities, the University of Sankore, was located in Timbuktu. After Musa made the city part of his empire, he turned the university into one of the most important centers of learning. At one point, Sankore was home to the largest library in the world.

Like many other rulers, Mansa Musa was dedicated to building large places of worship and monuments. He was a devout

Muslim and worked to spread his religion throughout his kingdom by building several magnificent mosques. Foreigners often visited Mali to admire the quality and style of the architecture.

In 1324, Mansa Musa traveled to Mecca on a pilgrimage. He took nearly 60,000 men with him, as well as huge amounts of gold in order to trade and show off Mali's wealth. He gave away millions of dollars' worth of gold on his journey. This caused problems for other kingdoms because they weren't prepared to be flooded with so much wealth. The traveling crew dressed in expensive silks. Naturally, Mansa Musa's travels caught the attention of many people. When he entered other empires, rulers made it a point to meet with him.

Mansa Musa is recognized as one of Africa's most influential rulers. He was likely one of the wealthiest men in the world during his reign.

> "This man flooded Cairo with his benefactions. He left no court emir nor holder of royal office without the gift of a load of gold."

—Arab historian Ibn Fadl All'h al-'Umari, speaking of Mansa Musa's pilgrimage

EXPLORE MORE!

You can watch an animated lesson about Mansa Musa by searching on ed.ted.com.

✳ QUEEN NZINGA ✳

c. 1583–1663

Queen Nzinga was a 17th-century African ruler. She is best remembered for setting her people free from slavery.

Anna Nzinga was born around 1583 into the royal family of Ndongo, which ruled the kingdom that is known today as Angola. As a child, she insisted on learning the military and political activities that usually only male children learned. She proved to be better than her brother and other children at using the battle ax, which was the royal symbol of her people. After her father, the king, died, her brother was selected as the new king. But Nzinga was smart and very skilled at making deals. Although her brother treated her poorly, he called on Nzinga to help negotiate with the Portuguese, who regularly invaded the kingdom and took prisoners as slaves. She was able to get the Portuguese to leave her land and instead trade with the kingdom as equals.

In 1624, she was chosen as the ruler after her brother passed away. Now in charge of the kingdom, Nzinga worked to improve and protect her territory at all costs. She was a fierce fighter and military leader, and she often led troops in battle.

In order to fight off the Portuguese, Nzinga made an alliance with the Dutch. As a woman, her right to the throne was constantly threatened. But Nzinga did not let this get in her way. Throughout her reign, Queen Nzinga used her shrewd mind and political ability to increase the territory and wealth of the kingdom.

Nzinga worked for the freedom and independence of her kingdom from the Portuguese. She was more successful than any other African ruler in resisting Portuguese rule. For this, she is called the "Mother of Angola" and the protector of her people. She is remembered today as a remarkable African woman who fought for freedom.

> **"**[She] lived an unmarried life just like the queen of the Amazons [and] she governed the army like a female warrior."

—A Jesuit missionary, speaking of Queen Nzinga

EXPLORE MORE!

Look for *The Egypt Game* by Zilpha Keatley Snyder to read an imaginative novel about three kids who invent a game about ancient Egypt that turns into a real mystery.

IGNATIUS SANCHO

1729–1780

gnatius Sancho was a British composer and writer. Although he was formerly enslaved, he taught himself to read and eventually spoke out against the slave trade.

Charles Ignatius Sancho was born in 1729 on a slave ship crossing the Atlantic Ocean headed to South America. Both of his parents died when he was a baby. As an orphan, he was brought to England, where he was enslaved and sold to three sisters. Later he worked for the Duke of Montagu. The Duke was impressed by Ignatius's wit and intelligence and gave him books to encourage his education. Ignatius taught himself to read and write.

Though it is unknown how, Ignatius became emancipated and was paid wages for his work. He continued to develop his skills in reading and writing and began speaking out against the slave trade. He also wrote music, poetry, and plays.

Ignatius was not only educated, he was well liked by the British elite, or wealthy, powerful people. After he left the English household, he and his wife opened a grocery store, where many politicians, writers, actors, and artists would gather. Ignatius became a successful businessman in his community. He got to know several leading politicians and did not shy away from offering his advice or opinions. He often wrote about politics and the economy, and he used his popularity to spread his message and share his views, especially against enslavement.

Ignatius began writing letters to abolitionists (people who wanted to end slavery), boldly criticizing the British for their part in the slave trade. Because he was so well respected, Ignatius remained a prominent figure in his community until his death in 1780.

"Alas! Time leaves the marks of his rough fingers upon all things."

EXPLORE MORE!

You can see scans of a book of Ignatius's letters published in 1784 at publicdomainreview.org.

BENJAMIN BANNEKER

1731–1806

Benjamin Banneker was a self-educated astronomer, mathematician, and writer. Among his achievements, he is known for helping establish the boundaries of Washington, D.C.

Benjamin Banneker was born in 1731 in Maryland. Both of his parents were free, so Benjamin was born free as well. As a child, Benjamin lived on a large farm and attended school when he could. When he couldn't go to school, he read as many books as he could. He especially liked science and math.

Benjamin's lack of schooling did not hold him back from learning. He had a brilliant mind, which he used to teach himself mathematics and astronomy, the study of outer space. In 1791, Benjamin was invited to help survey and design land that would become Washington, D.C. He worked with another man to build an observatory tent and use an instrument called a zenith sector to measure the movement of the stars.

Unfortunately, Benjamin's time with the surveying team was cut short when he became ill.

Benjamin Banneker is most well known for writing almanacs. An almanac is a yearly calendar that contains important seasonal dates as well as astronomical data, like the phases of the moon. With his almanacs, Benjamin was able to predict moon patterns, planet movements, and the daylight hours. His almanacs also included tables that showed the high and low tides. The tables were essential to sailors who transported goods using waterways, like rivers and canals.

Benjamin strongly believed that slavery should be abolished. In 1792, he wrote to future president Thomas Jefferson (who was secretary of state at the time) expressing his views. In his letter, he pointed out the injustice of white colonists in the United States wanting freedom from Britain while African Americans were enslaved. Benjamin also included a copy of his almanac to convince Jefferson that black people were capable of getting an education and achieving great things to benefit the country. Even though Jefferson was a slaveholder, he was impressed by Benjamin's achievements. Jefferson shared the almanac with others, and Benjamin gained the support of abolitionists in Maryland and Pennsylvania, who helped him continue to publish his almanacs.

"The colour of the skin is in no way connected with strength of the mind or intellectual powers."

EXPLORE MORE!

Check out the full text of Benjamin's letter to President Jefferson on pbs.org.

ABSALOM JONES

1746–1818

Absalom Jones was a minister and an activist. He was the first African American priest in the Episcopal Church in the United States.

Absalom Jones was born into slavery in Delaware in 1746. After moving to Philadelphia with his owner, he was allowed to attend school, where he learned to read and write. As an adult he married Mary King, who was also enslaved. He later paid for her freedom so their children would not be born into slavery. After purchasing his wife's freedom, Absalom asked his owner to grant him his own freedom. At first his owner refused, but eventually agreed to free him.

In 1780, Pennsylvania abolished slavery. In freedom, Absalom became a minister of St. George's Methodist Episcopal Church in Philadelphia. Though the church allowed people of all races to worship, it did not treat the African American members equally. Absalom was disgusted by the church's discrimination. He joined forces with another preacher named Richard Allen, and the two of them founded the Free African Society, an organization that helped widows, children, people who were sick, and others who needed assistance. The society dedicated itself to helping and raising up the black community.

Absalom wanted to start a black congregation that was separate from white control but was also part of the Episcopal Church. In 1794, he established the African Episcopal Church of St. Thomas, one of the first black congregations in Philadelphia. He became the first African American priest in the Episcopal Church.

Absalom was also a great speaker. He was known for his captivating speeches about black freedom and the struggles of African Americans. He played a role in starting a tradition of anti-slavery speeches on New Year's Day. He continued to speak out against slavery until his death in 1818.

"We implore thy blessing, O God, upon the President, and all who are in authority in the United States. Direct them by thy wisdom, in all their deliberations, and O save thy people from the calamities of war."

EXPLORE MORE!

You can find the full text of Absalom's first Thanksgiving speech on January 1, 1808, on the Project Canterbury website at anglicanhistory.org.

RICHARD ALLEN

1760–1831

Richard Allen was a minister, abolitionist, educator, and writer in Pennsylvania. He is best known as the founder of the African Methodist Episcopal Church.

Richard Allen was born into slavery in 1760, but as he grew up, he was determined to be free. In 1783, he bought his freedom for $2,000. Richard was an active member of the Methodist Church. He later joined St. George's Methodist Episcopal Church in Philadelphia, where he was an assistant minister for the black worshippers.

Over time, Richard became frustrated by the limitations put on him by the church. He was especially frustrated by how black parishioners were segregated in church, which means they had to sit in separate areas from white people. After much prayer and thought, Richard and other black members, including Absalom Jones, left the congregation. Richard and Absalom founded the Free African Society, a religious organization dedicated to helping the black community.

But Richard wanted to do more. His goal was to start an independent Methodist Church for African Americans. He founded Bethel Church in 1794. Years later, Bethel was combined with other churches to become the African Methodist Episcopal Church.

In 1830, Richard led a meeting of black church representatives from several states. The meeting was known as the National Negro Convention, or Colored Convention Movement. Its purpose was to address both local and national issues that affected free and enslaved African Americans. It was the largest meeting of its kind held by African Americans.

The Colored Convention Movement held meetings for more than three decades before and after the Civil War. These meetings led to the establishment of larger African American organizations, such as the Colored National Labor Union and the National Association for the Advancement of Colored People (NAACP). Today, the American Methodist Episcopal Church remains one of the most significant religious groups in the United States.

"The Lord was pleased to strengthen us, and remove all fear from us, and disposed our hearts to be as useful as possible."

EXPLORE MORE!

The AME denomination remains active today. Visit AME-church.com to learn more about their history and current work.

JAMES FORTEN

1766–1842

James Forten was an abolitionist and successful businessman. He used his wealth and social standing to fight for civil rights for African Americans.

James Forten was born free in 1766. He was a strong student but had to work to help support his family, especially after his father passed away in 1773. As a teenager, he fought in the Revolutionary War, but he was caught by the British and held as a prisoner.

After the war, James worked in Philadelphia as an apprentice for a sailmaker, which is a person who makes and repairs sails. James worked hard and became one of the best at his trade, even buying and taking over the business when the sailmaker retired. James developed a better sail that allowed ships to maneuver more accurately and with more speed. Ships that could travel quickly and successfully across oceans could help merchants make a lot of money, so they were willing to pay high prices for James's sails. In turn, James's business increased.

James hired both black and white workers at his company and paid them the same wages. He encouraged other businesses to do the same. As a successful businessman, James was able to use his status and wealth to fight for both enslaved and free African Americans. He opposed the American Colonization Society, which wanted to relocate freed African Americans to Liberia, a colony on the coast of Africa.

James purchased the freedom of some enslaved people. He also donated money to a newspaper called *The Liberator*, which advocated for the freedom of all enslaved people, and funded a school for black children. In addition, James allowed his home to be used as a stop on the Underground Railroad, which was a network of secret routes and houses used by enslaved African Americans to escape into free states.

James left behind a legacy of activism and philanthropy. For all his life, he embodied the ideals of the American Revolution—freedom, equality, and opportunity.

"It seems almost incredible that the advocates of liberty should conceive of the idea of selling a fellow creature to slavery."

EXPLORE MORE!

James Forten played a large role in abolishing slavery. Read his letters to other abolitionists by searching at digitalcommonwealth.org.

SHAKA ZULU

c. 1787–1828

Shaka Zulu was a famous African warrior and king. He was one of the most influential rulers of the Zulu Kingdom, which covered much of southern Africa.

Shaka Zulu was born around 1787. His father was a king of the Zulu nation, and his mother was a princess, the daughter of a rival king. Shaka's parents were not supposed to have had a child together because they were from different clans. Shaka and his mother were sent away from his father's clan to live with his mother's.

As a child, Shaka was often teased and ridiculed because of his family's history. However, over time he grew tall and strong. From an early age he was a natural leader. He became an expert fighter and military strategist. After the death of his father, Shaka Zulu became the leader of the Zulu Kingdom. He developed many new military tactics, which helped him gain power. For instance, his warriors used shorter spears, which gave them an advantage in hand-to-hand combat, and they fought with larger and stronger shields that offered more protection.

These new weapons and war strategies made Shaka's army very powerful.

Shaka Zulu is most remembered for his famous fighting strategy called the "buffalo horn formation." This three-part attack formation places the more experienced warriors in the center, or the chest, of the buffalo. Other soldiers form the horns of the buffalo. They surround the enemy, making it hard for them to escape. Under Shaka Zulu's rule, the Zulu nation expanded to include nearly 250,000 people plus an army of 50,000 men.

As king, Shaka Zulu became a respected leader by building friendships and relationships with neighboring clans in order to fight against larger tribes. Today, Shaka Zulu is still admired by the Zulu nation. His military strategies and rulership continue to be studied by historians and scholars.

> "I need no bodyguard at all, for even the bravest men who approach me get weak at the knees and their hearts turn to water."

EXPLORE MORE!

Shaka Zulu mastered several fighting styles. Research other ancient fighting styles like kung fu, jujutsu, and tae kwon do.

WILLIAM CUFFAY

1788–1870

William Cuffay was a politician and political activist. He was one of the leaders of the Chartist movement and a champion for workers' rights in Britain.

William Cuffay, the son of a formerly enslaved man and an English woman, was born in 1788 in Chatham, Kent, where his father worked as a cook on a warship. William was trained to be a tailor, but he also took an interest in politics. His political life began in 1834 when he and fellow workers organized a strike in support of tailors, who were forced to work long hours for low wages. Because he protested, he lost his job and could not find work anywhere.

William eventually joined the People's Charter movement. This was a political reform movement in Britain that had six demands, including that all men should have the right to vote and that members of parliament should not have to be property owners. William became determined to fight for equality in British society.

Before long, William became one of the leaders of a movement called Chartism, which took its name from the People's Charter. This was one of the largest political movements of the working class in Britain. Its main purpose was to bargain for better working conditions and treatment for employees. William was one of the only black men in his party, and he played a major role in the organization's growth.

William was one of three men who planned an uprising against the government. However, the plans were leaked to the authorities, so the uprising never took place. William was arrested, charged, convicted, and sentenced to 21 years in Tasmania, an island south of Australia. However, William's sentence did not stop him. When political prisoners were pardoned and allowed to leave Tasmania, William stayed. He worked as a tailor and continued his involvement in radical politics until he passed away in 1870. People today are still inspired by his commitment to supporting workers' rights.

> **"I say you have no right
> to sentence me."**

EXPLORE MORE!

Read *Kids on Strike!* by Susan Campbell Bartoletti to find out about children who worked in coal mines in the early 1900s—and how they found the bravery to go on strike to protest their inhumane working conditions.

SOJOURNER TRUTH

1797–1883

Sojourner Truth was an abolitionist and women's rights activist in the 1800s.

Sojourner Truth was born as Isabella Baumfree in 1797. She was born into slavery, and when she was only nine years old she was sold away from her parents. She married in 1815 and over time had five children. In 1826, after years of abuse, she escaped with her baby daughter to freedom.

Sojourner then began to work to free her other children from slavery. When she discovered that one of her sons had been sold to slaveholders in the South, she sued the slave owner and won freedom for her son. After a religious conversion in 1843, she gave herself the first name Sojourner, which means a person who travels, and the last name Truth. She chose this name because she believed she heard the voice of God telling her to preach the truth. She said, "Sojourner because I was to travel up and down the land showing people their sins and being a sign to them, and Truth because I was to declare the truth unto the people."

Sojourner began traveling around the north as a preacher and an abolitionist. She was a popular and powerful speaker. Although she never learned to read or write, she could vividly communicate the evils of slavery. Because of this, she was often invited to speak to large crowds.

Beyond her work to end slavery, Sojourner also advocated for women's rights. In 1851, she gave one of her most famous speeches, titled "Ain't I a Woman?" In the speech, she spoke bluntly about racism and gender inequality. The speech made her a leader in the early women's rights movement.

Sojourner later moved to Michigan, and when the Civil War started, she supported the Union Army in the north by calling for African Americans to enlist. She also worked with organizations that helped newly freed African Americans get settled. Today, Sojourner is recognized as a prominent historical figure in both the abolitionist and women's rights movements. Her work and dedication to both causes has been recognized in historic sites and public memorials.

"Life is a hard battle anyway. If we laugh and sing a little as we fight the good fight of freedom, it makes it all go easier. I will not allow my life's light to be determined by the darkness around me."

EXPLORE MORE!

Want to learn more about Sojourner Truth? Check out Kerri Lee Alexander's digital exhibit by searching at artsandculture.google.com.

MARY SEACOLE

1805–1881

Mary Seacole was a British Jamaican nurse who served during the Crimean War in Eastern Europe. She is famous for combining traditional herbal remedies with European medicine while nursing the British soldiers back to health.

Mary Seacole was born Mary Jane Grant in Jamaica in 1805. Her mother was a Jamaican healer, and her father was a Scottish officer. As a child, Mary learned about medicine from her mother, who ran a boarding house where she took care of injured soldiers. Mary liked to play nurse, caring for her dolls and pets. By the time she was 12, she was helping her mother care for patients, using traditional Caribbean remedies.

Mary spent time as a nurse in Panama, a country in Central America, where there was an outbreak of a disease called cholera. In 1851, she examined the body of a child who had died from cholera in order to understand the disease better. She was able to use her knowledge and skills to help other people suffering from cholera, and became known for her healing abilities.

In 1854, Mary volunteered to work as a nurse during the Crimean War but was rejected because of her race. But Mary knew her skills were needed, so she didn't give up. She saved money and paid her own way to the front lines of the war. Soon after she arrived, she set up what she called the British Hotel to care for the sick, recovering, hungry, cold, or any other soldiers who needed help. She was called "Mother Seacole" for her compassion and kindness.

After the war, Mary returned to England and published her memoir, *Wonderful Adventures of Mrs. Seacole in Many Lands*. She was in debt from the cost of the British Hotel, so the local newspapers started a fundraising campaign to support her. Mary's strength and determination had a lasting impact on the nursing industry. In 2004, she was voted the greatest black Briton. There is a statue of her on the grounds of St. Thomas' Hospital in London.

"Beside the nettle, ever grows the cure for its sting."

EXPLORE MORE!

You can find Mary Seacole's memoir, *Wonderful Adventures of Mrs. Seacole in Many Lands*, online. Read more about her fascinating life.

FREDERICK DOUGLASS

c. 1818–1895

Frederick Douglass was a renowned abolitionist, orator, politician, and activist.

Frederick Douglass was born into slavery in Maryland around 1818. He was separated from his mother as an infant. For a short time, he was raised by his maternal grandparents, but by the time he was six he was separated from his family again. In 1826, Frederick was given to new owners who lived in Baltimore, Maryland.

The slave owner's wife took a liking to him and decided to teach him the basics of reading. Unfortunately, her compassion did not last long. When her husband found out, he said that it would make Frederick unfit for slavery and they didn't let him read anymore. Frederick was forced to continue his education in secret since teaching enslaved African Americans to read was illegal. He would pick up lessons wherever he could, from eavesdropping on white children or reading any piece of writing that he could find. He eventually began to teach other enslaved African Americans to read.

Frederick felt that he had to escape slavery in order to survive. One day he made a promise to himself that he would escape by the end of the year. He made a plan with several other enslaved people, but someone reported them and they were prevented from escaping. However, in 1838 Frederick did successfully escape and head north. A few years later he married and moved to Massachusetts. As a free man, Frederick began his life's work of opposing slavery. He was a masterful speaker, and he traveled throughout the United States educating northerners on the brutality of slavery. In 1845, he published his first autobiography, which was read around the world. For nearly two years he traveled through England and Ireland.

When Frederick returned to the United States, he began to publish *The North Star*, an abolitionist newspaper. When the Civil War began, he successfully advocated for the enlistment of African Americans in the Union Army. He also began to call for the right to vote for African Americans and for women. After the war, Frederick continued to demand equal rights for everyone. He became the foremost black leader in the United States.

"I have often been utterly astonished, since I came to the north, to find persons who could speak of the singing, among slaves, as evidence of their contentment and happiness. It is impossible to conceive of a greater mistake."

EXPLORE MORE!

Frederick Douglass was a master orator. Read his speeches at frederickdouglass.org.

HARRIET TUBMAN

c. 1822–1913

Harriet Tubman was a freedom fighter and abolitionist. After she escaped slavery, she led dozens of other enslaved people to freedom along the route of the Underground Railroad.

Harriet Tubman was born as Araminta Ross around the year 1822. She lived on a plantation with her parents and siblings, but the family was split up, with different members sold to different plantations. She worked as a house servant from an early age—as young as five or six. Throughout her childhood, Harriet was brutally beaten and abused by the slave owners. These horrific events instilled in Harriet a desperate desire to be free.

Harriet constantly planned her escape, despite knowing that there could be violent consequences. In 1849, she ran away to Pennsylvania, a free state. She worked and lived as a free woman in the city of Philadelphia, but Harriet's own freedom was not enough for her. She wanted her whole family to be free.

Harriet knew that if she returned to save her family, she would be putting herself in danger and could even be enslaved again. Her friends in Philadelphia warned her to be cautious. But in 1850, she left Philadelphia to rescue her family. Over the next few years Harriet led more than 70 people to freedom along the Underground Railroad.

Even as slavery ended, Harriet continued fighting for freedom. When the Civil War started, she joined the Union Army and worked as a nurse. The soldiers noticed that she was familiar with the land and the people. They also knew that Harriet was a great organizer and leader. She was called on to lead an important Union raid on the enemy territory. She became the first woman in history to lead a military raid.

Harriet dedicated her life to ending slavery and leading others to freedom. She did everything she could to help others, giving away money and property even though she was living in poverty. Her bravery and determination not only helped her to free many people, but also to expose the injustice of enslavement.

"I was the conductor of the Underground Railroad for eight years, and I can say what most conductors can't say—I never ran my train off the track and I never lost a passenger."

EXPLORE MORE!

Look for *Eliza's Freedom Road: An Underground Railroad Diary* by Jerdine Nolen to read a historical novel about an enslaved girl's journey to freedom.

REBECCA LEE CRUMPLER

1831–1895

Rebecca Lee Crumpler was the first African American woman in the United States to become a doctor.

Rebecca Lee Crumpler was born Rebecca Davis in Delaware in 1831. She learned about medicine from her aunt, who often cared for sick neighbors. In school, Rebecca was described as a "special student in mathematics." Once she finished school, she worked as a nurse for various doctors for several years.

Rebecca was accepted to the New England Female Medical College in 1860. This was the first medical college for women in the world. At the time, many white male doctors looked down on the school and mocked the idea of women as doctors. They believed women were incapable of practicing medicine and that studying human anatomy was inappropriate for women's "sensitive and delicate nature." But Rebecca knew she had the strength, experience, and talent for a career in medicine, so she pushed forward with her education.

While in medical school, Rebecca faced harsh racism. Faculty and administrators did not want her to pass because they felt she had not shown enough progress. Despite this, Rebecca graduated in 1864. She was the first African American woman to earn a Doctor of Medicine degree.

After she graduated, Rebecca practiced medicine in Boston. She followed her aunt's example and took care of the people who needed her help the most, particularly African American women and children living in poverty. In 1865, after the Civil War, she moved to Virginia, where she worked for the Freedmen's Bureau providing medical care to newly freed slaves.

Rebecca used her career to spread knowledge. In 1883, she published *A Book of Medical Discourses*. The book focused on women and children's health and talked about many common medical issues that mothers experienced. This book was one of the first written by an African American about medicine.

Rebecca's legacy continues to inspire others to pursue their goals in medicine. One of the first medical societies for black women is named in her honor: the Rebecca Lee Society. Her old home in Boston is now a stop on the Women's Heritage Trail.

"It may be well to state here that, having been reared by a kind aunt in Pennsylvania, whose usefulness with the sick was continually sought, I early conceived a liking for, and sought every opportunity to relieve the sufferings of others."

EXPLORE MORE!

Search online or at your local library to learn about the first African American nurse, Mary Eliza Mahoney, and other early pioneers in medicine.

GEORGE
* WASHINGTON *
CARVER

c. 1860–1943

George Washington Carver was a renowned scientist, inventor, and educator. He was the most prominent African American scientist of the early 20th century.

George Washington Carver was born into slavery in Missouri. While he was an infant, he, a sister, and their mother were kidnapped and sold to a slaveholder in Kentucky. George alone was returned to his former owner in Missouri.

Thereafter, George and his other siblings were raised by a slave owner. The family taught George how to read and write. He would remain dedicated to education despite many obstacles. Black people weren't allowed to attend the nearby school, so every day he traveled nearly 10 miles to school. His determination paid off, and he eventually graduated high school.

After high school, George began to study botany. He was the first black student at Iowa Agricultural College (now called Iowa State University). George proved to be a gifted botanist, and many of his teachers encouraged him to continue to graduate school. In 1896, he was recruited by prominent African American leader Booker T. Washington to lead the agriculture department at Tuskegee Institute.

George's research showed farmers new ways to keep their soil healthy by planting crops other than cotton, including peanuts. His study transformed the industry. Throughout the South, farmers began to plant and use peanuts in new ways. George became the most well-known scientist in the country. He not only promoted the use of the peanuts for agricultural purposes, but he also created several recipes and products that showed how the food source could be successfully used.

George's work in botany dramatically increased peanut production in the United States. His work gained respect from politicians and scientists, both at home and abroad. His work continues to influence the food, agriculture, and botany fields.

"When you can do the common things of life in an uncommon way, you will command the attention of the world."

EXPLORE MORE!

George Washington Carver discovered more than 300 ways to use the peanut. You can find a list on the Tuskegee University website at tuskegee.edu.

IDA B. WELLS-BARNETT

1862–1931

I da B. Wells-Barnett was an investigative journalist and activist. Her newspaper stories about lynchings in the South made her a civil rights pioneer.

Ida Bell Wells-Barnett was born in Holly Springs, Mississippi, in 1862. She was born into slavery but was freed when President Abraham Lincoln issued the Emancipation Proclamation in 1863, ending slavery in the United States. Ida's parents taught her the importance of education. She attended Rust College, which still exists today.

Ida's education was cut short when her parents and one of her siblings died in a yellow fever epidemic, leaving Ida to care for her remaining siblings. She found a job as a teacher to make money and, after her brothers became carpentry apprentices, moved with her sisters to Memphis, Tennessee.

In Tennessee, Ida wrote articles about injustice for her church newspapers. Her first story was about an experience of her own. A train company had forced her to leave the train because she was not sitting in the car reserved for black customers, even though Ida had bought a first-class ticket. When Ida refused to leave her seat, she was physically removed from the train. In 1884, she filed a lawsuit against the company and was awarded $500. She published an article about the experience in a newspaper under the name "Lola." She was later given the title "Lola, Princess of the Press."

When one of Ida's friends was lynched (a type of murder that almost always targets black people), Ida began to research acts of violence against black people in the South in order to educate others. She wrote powerful articles on the topic and boldly published her findings in local newspapers. Her work enraged many racists, who burned her press and forced her out of Memphis. Ida continued with her mission despite these dangerous obstacles. In 1898, she visited the White House to meet with President William McKinley to try to convince him to take action against lynchings.

Ida B. Wells-Barnett remains one of the most important leaders of the early civil rights movement. Her activism was an inspiration to journalists who came after her.

"The very frequent inquiry made after my lectures by interested friends is 'What can I do to help the cause?' The answer always is: 'Tell the world the facts.'"

EXPLORE MORE!

Learn more about Ida B. Wells-Barnett by reading *The Princess of the Press* by Angela Shelf Medearis.

MAGGIE LENA WALKER

1864–1934

Maggie Lena Walker was an entrepreneur, businesswoman, and philanthropist. She was the first African American woman to charter a bank.

Maggie Lena Walker was born in Virginia in 1864. She grew up very poor and had to help her family by working with her mother in a laundry business.

Maggie attended a local school in Richmond, Virginia, and became a teacher after graduation. When she was a teenager, she joined the Independent Order of St. Luke (IOSL), an African American organization that helped sick and elderly people. She held many top leadership positions there, including the role of grand deputy matron and grand secretary. In 1902, she began publishing the organization's newspaper, *The St. Luke Herald*. She also started a department store, called the St. Luke Emporium, where black women could find jobs and learn to work in retail.

Maggie was very good at accounting and math. In 1903, she founded the St. Luke Penny Savings Bank. She was the first woman of any race to charter a bank in the United States. She also encouraged children to save money by passing out penny banks.

Maggie lost her husband in 1915, which left her in charge of a large estate. Even so, she continued working for the IOSL and other civic organizations, including the National Association of Colored Women (NACW), which had the slogan "Lifting as We Climb," and sought to improve life for all African Americans. She also served as the vice president of the Richmond chapter of the National Association for the Advancement of Colored People (NAACP).

Maggie's house in Richmond, Virginia, was made a National Historic Site by the National Park Service. Through her work and her passion, she paved the way for other African Americans to be business leaders in their communities.

> **❝** I was not born with a silver spoon in my mouth, but with a laundry basket practically on my head.**"**

EXPLORE MORE!

Learn more about Maggie Lena Walker at the National Museum of American History website: americanhistory.si.edu.

MADAM C.J. WALKER

1867–1919

Madam C.J. Walker was a wealthy businesswoman and philanthropist. She built a hair-care products business that made her one of the first American women to become a millionaire.

Madam C.J. Walker was born Sarah Breedlove in 1867 in Louisiana. Both of her parents died when she was young, and she was raised by her older sister. As a child, Sarah worked as a domestic servant to earn money. Her work often prevented her from attending school. In 1888, Sarah moved to St. Louis, Missouri, with her daughter.

In St. Louis, Sarah worked hard washing laundry for a dollar a day to escape poverty and provide for her daughter. She noticed that the hair and beauty market excluded African American women. Some African American women washed their hair with a chemical called lye, which could burn the scalp. So, with her brothers who were barbers, Sarah started working on her own product line aimed at the hair concerns of black women. She began to sell her products door to door and later moved to mail orders.

In 1908, Sarah moved to Pittsburgh and opened her own beauty parlor. There, she began to train other women on her grooming and product-promotion techniques. She mainly employed black women who, like her, wanted to escape poverty. This successful network of women worked throughout the United States, and the products were sold everywhere.

Sarah soon became the wealthiest African American businesswoman in the country. But she was not only interested in making money. She also used her wealth to advance social and political issues. She frequently gave large donations to black organizations and causes. After Sarah died in 1919, her daughter, A'Lelia Walker, continued her work and legacy.

Sarah's products and business ideas transformed the beauty industry. Today, her work continues to inspire entrepreneurs and businesswomen to reach for the stars.

> "Don't sit down and wait for the opportunities to come. Get up and make them."

EXPLORE MORE!

You can read about Madam C.J. Walker's mentor, Annie Turnbo Malone, and other important women in black history in *Black Women in Science: A Black History Book for Kids* by Kimberly Brown Pellum.

W.E.B. DU BOIS

1868–1963

W.E.B. Du Bois was an intellectual, philosopher, and civil rights activist. He was one of the founders of the NAACP.

William Edward Burghardt Du Bois was born in 1868 in Massachusetts. As a child, he attended an integrated school, which means it had both black and white students. At a young age, he proved to be a strong student. Although he grew up in an integrated community, he still experienced racism. He never forgot his encounters with discrimination and racism.

In 1885, the Du Bois family pooled together funds from neighbors to send him to Fisk University, a historically black university in Nashville, Tennessee. After graduating, he enrolled at Harvard University, where he studied history and sociology. He also earned a fellowship to study in Germany. William used his time abroad to study international politics and social history. In 1895, he became the first African American to earn a PhD from Harvard.

After graduating, William took a teaching position in Ohio. After two years there, he accepted a position at the University of Pennsylvania, where he began to research and work on a sociology study called *The Philadelphia Negro*. This would be one of his many projects that centered on African American life and history.

In 1900, William attended the First Pan-African Conference, which was held in London. The conference called for a halt to European imperialism in Africa, which had to do with Europeans trying to take over countries in Africa. He also wanted to put an end to the racism that African Americans faced. In 1905, he joined other African American leaders to create the Niagara Movement, which opposed racial segregation. The organization eventually morphed into the NAACP (National Association for the Advancement of Colored People). The NAACP would be one of the primary organizations that eventually ended segregation.

Throughout his life, William remained an activist and scholar, publishing many works on the lives of African Americans. Today, his work is still recognized for offering a groundbreaking analysis of race in the United States.

"Children learn more from what you are than what you teach."

EXPLORE MORE!

Read *Little Legends: Exceptional Men in Black History* by Vashti Harrison to be introduced to other inspiring figures.

CARTER G. WOODSON

1875–1950

Carter G. Woodson was a scholar, historian, and journalist. He founded Black History Month and is known as the "Father of Black History."

Carter G. Woodson was born in Virginia in 1875. Both of his parents were formerly enslaved. For most of his childhood, Carter was unable to attend school regularly because the family was extremely poor. In order to help out and to make money for his family, he worked on the family farm and in the coal mines. Carter's father encouraged him to be kind and respectful to others, but also to expect respect in return.

When Carter was able to go to class, he was a good student. He continued to fight hard for his education, going on to graduate from Berea College in Kentucky, then attend the University of Chicago and Harvard University. He became the second African American to receive a PhD from Harvard. (The first was W.E.B. Du Bois.)

Carter continued his long career in education, working in public schools in Washington, D.C., and as the dean of the College of Arts and Sciences at Howard University, a historically black college. He had a great passion for promoting the study of African American history, which was overlooked and not valued at the time. To this end, he started the Association for the Study of Negro Life and History in 1915. The goal of the organization was to give black scholars opportunities to study black history and to publish their work.

In 1916, Carter began to publish a journal called *The Journal of Negro History*, which is still being published today (now called *The Journal of African American History*). He also wrote many important books, including *The Mis-Education of the Negro*. In this book, he argued that schools in the United States conditioned black people to accept a low status in society and to not take pride in their heritage. The book is still taught in universities today.

Carter's lifelong goal of advancing the study of black history was realized when he successfully fought for public schools to dedicate one week per year as Negro History Week. Carter's legacy is clear. The week he envisioned eventually became a month, known as Black History Month, which is still celebrated every February to this day.

> "The mere imparting of information is not education. Above all things, the effort must result in making a man think and do for himself."

EXPLORE MORE!

Learn more about Carter Woodson at the website for the Association for the Study of African American Life and History at asalh.org.

MARY McLEOD BETHUNE

1875–1955

Mary McLeod Bethune was an educator, political leader, and philanthropist.

Mary McLeod was born in South Carolina in 1875. Her parents were formerly enslaved, and she was one of 17 children. Mary was the only one of her siblings to go to school. She walked miles to the schoolhouse every day, and at night she would teach her family what she had learned.

Mary won a scholarship to Scotia Seminary, a school for black girls in North Carolina. She later went to Moody Bible Institute with the goal of traveling to Africa as a missionary. When she was told there were no openings for black missionaries, she turned her attention to becoming a teacher.

Mary married Albertus Bethune, who was also a teacher, and settled in Daytona, Florida, where she set out to open her own school. She started the Daytona Normal and Industrial Institute for Negro Girls in 1904. Mary worked tirelessly to make money for the school. Over the years it changed from an elementary school to a high school, then a junior college to a college. Today, the private, historically black school is called Bethune–Cookman University.

Mary also became known as a leader in the fight for civil rights and equality for African Americans and women. She used her powerful voice to inform others about the need for education, housing, food, and employment in the black community. She also created the National Council of Negro Women (NCNW). The NCNW pushed for the advancement of African American women in all fields.

Mary's work eventually caught the attention of the White House. First Lady Eleanor Roosevelt was drawn to Mary's success and selected her to be a part of a small group of black leaders who regularly advised President Franklin D. Roosevelt on civil rights issues. Today there is a statue of her in Washington, D.C., with an inscription that reads, in part, "I leave you love. I leave you hope . . . I leave you a thirst for education."

"The whole world opened up to me when I learned to read."

EXPLORE MORE!

Read more about Mary McLeod Bethune and Bethune-Cookman University at cookman.edu.

ERNEST JUST

1883–1941

Ernest Just was a biologist, educator, and science writer. He was a pioneer in our understanding of cellular biology.

Ernest Everett Just was born in 1883 in South Carolina. His father passed away when Ernest was a child. He was raised by his mother, who worked as a teacher to support the family. At the age of six, Ernest contracted a disease called typhoid fever. Though he recovered, he lost parts of his memory and motor skills. He had to work hard to learn to read and write again.

Schools for black people in the South did not have the same resources as schools for white people, so Ernest went to New Hampshire for high school. He was the only black student in his class. Ernest's mother passed away during his time there. Though he was devastated, he continued to work hard and graduated a year early.

Ernest went on to attend Dartmouth College, where he took a keen interest in zoology and botany. At Dartmouth, Ernest became fascinated with cell biology. Every summer he went to the Marine Biological Laboratory in Massachusetts, where he

studied the cells of marine worms and other small sea crea-
tures. He made observations about how eggs are fertilized that
went against what scientists thought at the time. Scientists
around the world began to pay attention to his work.

But despite his achievements, Ernest was not treated the
same as white scientists in the United States. He moved to
France, where he continued his work and published groundbreaking books. Throughout his life, Ernest never lost his
curiosity about the natural world or his passion for sharing it
with others. His innovative research in cell structure is often
cited in scientific studies today.

"We feel the beauty of Nature because we are part of Nature and because we know that however much in our separate domains we abstract from the unity of Nature, this unity remains."

EXPLORE MORE!

Are you curious about science like Ernest was? Look for a book of science experiments, like *Awesome Science Experiments for Kids* by Crystal Chatterton, to start learning!

ZORA NEALE HURSTON

1891–1960

Zora Neale Hurston was an author and anthropologist. She was a prolific writer, best known for her novel *Their Eyes Were Watching God.*

Zora Neale Hurston was born in 1891 in Alabama. Her family moved to Eatonville, Florida, while Zora was young. Eatonville was one of the many all-black towns in the South, and Zora's father was one of the town's first mayors. Zora's early childhood in Eatonville was a mostly happy time. She was a spirited girl, and though her father often tried to tame her behavior, her mother encouraged her to "jump at the sun." Unfortunately, Zora's mother passed away when Zora was 13, and she spent her later childhood living with various family members.

Years later, Zora attended Howard University, where she cofounded the student newspaper, *The Hilltop*. She won a scholarship to Barnard College in New York City. Her move to New York was a pivotal event in her life, as it put her on the road to literary greatness.

In New York, Zora made friends with other well-known African American writers, such as Langston Hughes. Together, they started a magazine called *FIRE!!*. Zora and her friends became part of the Harlem Renaissance, a period of artistic and creative growth filled with new music, writing, and art in black culture.

Zora wrote passionately and authentically about African American experiences. She traveled abroad to study black religions and cultures, and often used what she learned in her writing. She published three books between 1934 and 1939. One of her most popular was *Their Eyes Were Watching God*. This novel is about the tumultuous life of a girl named Janie Crawford, who searches for a sense of identity. Zora was one of the first authors to focus her work on the experiences of a black woman.

Zora Neale Hurston's literary work was groundbreaking. Her contributions have had a lasting effect on black social and cultural arts.

"Sometimes I feel discriminated against, but it does not make me angry. It merely astonishes me. How can any deny themselves the pleasure of my company? It's beyond me."

EXPLORE MORE!

Throughout her career, Zora Neale Hurston researched and documented many African fables and tales. Enjoy some of her favorites in *What's the Hurry, Fox? And Other Animal Stories*.

BESSIE COLEMAN

1892–1926

Bessie Coleman was a world-famous aviator and social activist. She was the first black woman to hold a pilot's license.

Bessie Coleman was born in 1892 in Atlanta, Texas. She grew up poor and often worked alongside her mother to earn money for her and her 12 siblings. Like many black Southern families at the time, Bessie's family made their living picking cotton. Bessie enjoyed reading and had an active imagination, but she was unable to finish her education when she ran out of money for tuition.

In 1915, Bessie moved to Chicago to live with her brothers. She enrolled in cosmetology school and started working as a manicurist in a barbershop. She soon became known as the best manicurist in black Chicago. In Chicago, Bessie often met World War I soldiers who would talk about the thrill and excitement of flying planes. She was inspired to try to get a pilot's license herself. Unfortunately, flight schools in the United States allowed neither women nor black people. Instead of giving up, Bessie decided to go to aviation school in France!

Bessie took a boat to France and was accepted to the Caudron Brothers' School of Aviation. In 1921, she became the first woman to earn a pilot's license and the first African American to earn an international pilot's license. She quickly became a media sensation.

Bessie excelled at stunt flying, performing dangerous tricks for large audiences. She soared through the air, exciting the crowds with figure eights and loops. Bessie had a lot of fans, and she made sure to use her popularity and her voice to promote equality. She refused to perform in front of segregated audiences, and she spoke openly about the inequalities that African Americans faced. She made plans to open a flight school with hopes of training more black aviators.

Though Bessie didn't live to see the dream of her flight school come true, her legacy continues to soar. By 1977, a group of black female pilots formed the Bessie Coleman Aviators Club, and in 1995, the US Postal Service released the Bessie Coleman stamp. Every year, on the anniversary of Bessie's death, African American pilots fly over her grave and drop flowers in her honor.

> "You tell the world
> I'm coming back!"

EXPLORE MORE!

Check out all the African American heritage stamps offered at the United States Postal Service. Head to an office near you or find them at usps.com.

BESSIE SMITH

1894–1937

Bessie Smith was a famous singer and entertainer. She was the most popular female blues singer of the 1920s and 1930s.

Bessie Smith was born in 1894 in Tennessee. Before she was nine years old, Bessie lost her father, mother, and a brother. Her older sister, Viola, took over the family. The remaining family—now Bessie, Viola, and brothers Andrew and Clarence—struggled to make ends meet.

In order to make money, Bessie and her brother Andrew took to performing in the streets. Her brother Clarence joined a traveling show, and a few years later, Bessie followed his lead, working as a dancer. Bessie was mentored by another famous African American singer named Ma Rainey. Rainey taught Bessie how to command the stage with emotion and power.

In 1923, Bessie began her recording career as a singer. Her music immediately became popular with African Americans. She mostly performed and recorded the blues. Bessie's music illuminated the hardships of working-class African Americans in the

South. She was not afraid to discuss issues of racism, income inequality, and gender.

Bessie had a recognizable and passionate voice that drew listeners to her. Her shows were well attended by many who identified with her music and life. Her adoring fans and reviewers gave her the title "Empress of the Blues." During the height of her career, Bessie was the highest-paid African American entertainer. Her intense travel schedule called for her to use a private train car, which was unheard of for a black person during the racially segregated era. Throughout her career, Bessie recorded nearly 160 songs and performances. She also starred in a film and in one Broadway play.

When Bessie passed away in 1937, many people attended her funeral. An estimated 10,000 mourners paid their respects. But despite her popularity, her grave remained unmarked until 1970 when Bessie's friends and other musicians paid for a tombstone.

Since 1983, three of Bessie's recordings have been added to the Grammy Hall of Fame. The induction is a testimony of Bessie's influence and significance as a musician. Today, she is recognized as one of the greatest singers of the blues and jazz era.

> **"I don't want no drummer. I set the tempo."**

EXPLORE MORE!

You can check out Bessie Smith's songs wherever you get your music. Start with one of her most famous, "Backwater Blues."

PAUL ROBESON

1898–1976

Paul Robeson was a singer, actor, and political activist. Though some saw his activism as controversial, he remained true to his beliefs throughout his life.

Paul Robeson was born in New Jersey in 1898. His mother was a Quaker teacher. His father had been enslaved in North Carolina but escaped, went to university, and became a Presbyterian minister. However, Paul's father resigned from the ministry after facing discrimination from some white parishioners. In 1903, Paul lost his mother in a house fire.

A few years later, the family moved to Somerville, New Jersey, and Paul became a star student and athlete. It was during this time that he fell in love with acting. Paul performed in several Shakespeare productions and, after graduating, received a scholarship to Rutgers University. Paul was only the third African American to attend the school. He graduated as valedictorian from Rutgers and went on to attend Columbia Law School.

Paul worked as a lawyer for only a few months before he was driven out by the law firm's racism. In 1924, he began acting full time in professional productions. He starred in several hit plays, including Eugene O'Neill's *All God's Chillun Got Wings*. He received a recording contract and began a long career of reviving African American spirituals, or religious folk songs. Paul also acted in films and was given starring roles, which was uncommon for black actors at the time.

Throughout his career, Paul was an outspoken advocate for civil rights in Europe, Africa, and Asia as well as the United States. During World War II, he supported the American troops by organizing several benefit concerts. But despite his patriotism, he was often investigated by the federal government. Many of his concerts were canceled, and he was barred from traveling out of the country. The press regularly attacked Paul, which further hurt his career.

While the setbacks Paul endured were harsh, his legacy remains. He was a powerful performer and person and used his many talents to fight for justice for disadvantaged people around the world.

> **"The answer to injustice is not to silence the critic but to end the injustice."**

EXPLORE MORE!

Listen to the podcast "'Ol' Man River': An American Masterpiece" to learn more about Paul Robeson and hear him sing.

DUKE ELLINGTON

1899–1974

Duke Ellington was a renowned composer and musician. He is considered one of the greatest jazz composers of all time.

Duke Ellington was born in 1899 in Washington, D.C. Music was part of his life from the beginning. Both of his parents were talented pianists, and they often entertained Duke with their music. He began taking music lessons at the age of seven. Although he enjoyed the lessons, he also loved baseball and even took a job as a peanut salesman at the local stadium.

As a teenager, Duke rediscovered his passion for playing the piano. He would sneak into clubs to hear the "rag-time" sound. Ragtime was an up-and-coming style of music created by African Americans. Inspired by ragtime's unique sound, Duke dedicated his life to being a musician. He wrote his first composition, "Soda Fountain Rag," when he was still a teenager.

In 1927, he started to play at New York's world-famous Cotton Club in Harlem. He not only played the piano, but he also directed the 11-piece band. Although he was the main attraction, Duke let other band members shine. Every musician showed off their own style. This was an innovation in the big-band music style and part of what made Duke a jazz legend.

Duke's music was admired around the world. The Ellington Orchestra often traveled around Europe, playing to packed venues of eager crowds. Back in the United States, however, Duke's tours sometimes took him through the South, which was still segregated. But this didn't stop Duke from taking his performances to his fans. He also showed his talent in films and onstage. He cowrote a musical show called *Chocolate Kiddies*, which starred legendary actress Josephine Baker.

Duke Ellington masterfully blended classical music and jazz in order to create a new sound. He was a one-of-a-kind musician, and one of the most influential people in the history of jazz.

"Music, of course, is what I hear and something that I more or less live by. It's not an occupation or profession, it's a compulsion."

EXPLORE MORE!

Seek out Duke Ellington's songs on whatever music service you use. Start with one of his best known: "It Don't Mean a Thing (If It Ain't Got That Swing)."

FUNMILAYO RANSOME-KUTI

1900–1978

Funmilayo Ransome-Kuti was a Nigerian activist, teacher, and political leader. She fought tirelessly to give women in Africa access to education and representation in government.

Funmilayo Ransome-Kuti was born Frances Abigail Olufunmilayo Thomas in 1900 in Nigeria, a country in West Africa. Her parents believed in equal education for boys and girls, and she was one of the first women to attend Abeokuta Grammar School. She continued her studies in England from 1919 to 1922 before coming home and taking a teaching job at the same school she had attended as a girl.

In 1944, Funmilayo started the Abeokuta Ladies Club (ALC), an organization for educated women who wanted to help others. Two years later it changed its name to the Abeokuta Women's Union (AWU) and became more powerful. The AWU welcomed all women, whether they were educated or not, in order to protect women who worked in outdoor community markets. It defended the women when the government started taking their rice without paying them for it.

The AWU continued to grow and fight for more causes. Funmilayo and the AWU fought for women's rights, demanded that women be represented in local government, and worked to end the unfair taxes that market women were forced to pay. Funmilayo led marches and protests of up to 10,000 people, and even forced the ruling party to resign in 1949. People began to call her the "Lioness of Lisabi."

Funmilayo had a long list of political achievements over her lifetime. She helped to create the Nigerian Women's Union (NWU) and the Federation of Nigerian Women's Societies (FNWS). She also founded the Commoners People's Party, and she was the first woman to be elected to the House of Chiefs. Funmilayo Ransome-Kuti was a powerful and outspoken leader who never backed down from demanding rights for women.

> " As for the charges against me, I am unconcerned. I am beyond their timid lying morality and so I am beyond caring."

EXPLORE MORE!

Look for John Adoga's Nigerian history book series to find out more about Funmilayo Ransome-Kuti and other Nigerian leaders.

LANGSTON HUGHES

1902–1967

Langston Hughes was a renowned poet and playwright as well as a social activist. He is best known for being a leading figure of the Harlem Renaissance.

James Mercer Langston Hughes was born in 1902 in Missouri and was raised by his grandmother in Lawrence, Kansas. His grandmother raised him to take great pride in his race. As a child, Langston loved reading. Books gave him an escape from his ordinary life. He started writing when he was very young and was made "class poet" in eighth grade. He wrote his first poem for the graduation ceremony.

As a teenager, Langston treasured literature. He began writing for the school newspaper and started to write poetry regularly. One of his first major poems, "The Negro Speaks of Rivers," was published in a magazine called *The Crisis* in 1921. Two years later, Langston left to explore the world. He traveled to Africa and Spain, and lived in England and Paris for a short time before returning to the United States to finish college.

Langston lived in Harlem, New York, in the 1920s and 1930s. This was during the Harlem Renaissance—an explosion of intellectual and artistic growth in the black community, with more black musicians, writers, and artists than anywhere in the world. Langston was inspired by the energy of the time and place, and his writing blossomed. He published "Let America Be America Again" in 1936. This powerful poem expressed the hopes and dreams of black people in the United States and remains one of his most celebrated works.

Langston wrote stories and poems that shed light on African Americans in a new way, exploring their every-day lives. He wrote plays and even worked to develop films. Langston also mentored other black writers by starting writing groups and theater troupes. The organizations groomed many up-and-coming writers and playwrights, helping to launch their careers. Today, Langston's powerful novels and poems continue to connect readers to African American experiences.

> " Jazz, to me, is one of the inherent expressions of negro life in America: The eternal tom-tom beating in the negro soul—the tom-tom of revolt against weariness in a white world . . . the tom-tom of joy and laughter, and pain swallowed in a smile."

EXPLORE MORE!

You can listen to Langston reading his poems online, or read his poetry in *Poetry for Young People: Langston Hughes* edited by David Roessel.

RALPH JOHNSON BUNCHE

1904–1971

Ralph Bunche was a political scientist and diplomat. He was the first African American to win the Nobel Peace Prize.

Ralph Johnson Bunche was born in 1904 in Michigan. He was a talented athlete and student and graduated as valedictorian from both high school and college. He later studied political science at Harvard University and became the first African American to receive a PhD in that field.

Ralph taught at Howard University for nearly 25 years and founded the school's political science department. He was a brilliant scholar and a careful researcher. He traveled extensively in French West Africa in the 1930s and returned with fascinating insights on segregation in the region. He also published a booklet titled *A World View of Race*, which shared new ideas about race.

In 1936, Ralph helped start the National Negro Congress, which brought together African American leaders from many fields to fight for labor and civil rights. He also contributed to a study done by a Swedish sociologist (a scientist who studies human society) about race relations between black people and white people in the United States. The study was published as *An American Dilemma: The Negro Problem and Modern Democracy.*

Along with Ralph's work as a scholar, he was an important figure in the civil rights movement. He participated in the 1963 March on Washington as well as the Selma to Montgomery Voting Rights March, a mass protest in which people walked for three days from Selma to Montgomery, Alabama.

In the mid-1940s, Ralph began the most important project of his career when he went to the Middle East to help negotiations between Arabs and Jews in Palestine. He worked with great patience and humanity to encourage both sides to compromise. Some negotiations even took place while playing pool! After many months, Ralph was able to arrange a cease-fire (an agreement to stop fighting) between the two groups. He won the Nobel Peace Prize for his accomplishment, becoming the first African American to achieve that honor.

Ralph received many other awards for his work, including the Presidential Medal of Freedom. He is remembered for his intelligence, optimism, and dedication to worldwide peace.

"To make our way, we must have firm resolve, persistence, tenacity. We must gear ourselves to work hard all the way. We can never let up."

EXPLORE MORE!

Visit nobelprize.org to read about other inspiring people honored with the award.

JOSEPHINE BAKER

1906–1975

Josephine Baker was a world-renowned performer and activist. She worked in the French Resistance during World War II, and was devoted to fighting segregation in the United States.

Josephine Baker was born Freda Josephine McDonald in St. Louis, Missouri, in 1906. Both of her parents were entertainers, and as a child, Josephine was often invited onstage to perform. It was there that she began to fall in love with the spotlight. Her parents' careers didn't make much money, however, so Josephine had to take odd jobs to help her family out. She would often collect money for dancing on the street.

Josephine's dance routine caught the attention of an African American theater troupe, and at age 15, she ran off to perform with the group. She married a man named Willie Baker, took his last name, and dropped her first name to become Josephine Baker. She kept the name the rest of her life.

Josephine flourished as a dancer. When she was 19, she went to Paris to perform in an all-black review. She became one of the most sought-after performers because of her distinct dancing style and creative costumes. Her dancing was energetic and improvisational and reflected African themes and styles. She was multitalented, known for both dancing and singing, and she even appeared in several successful movies in Europe.

When World War II started, Josephine joined the French Resistance to fight against the Nazi regime. She helped French military officials by sharing confidential information she picked up when Nazis came to see her performances. She wrote the secrets in invisible ink on sheet music to keep from getting caught.

In the United States, Josephine was also a civil rights activist, even participating in the March on Washington with Martin Luther King Jr. in 1963. She continued this activism for the rest of her life. In her final performance in 1975, the show was sold out, and she received a standing ovation. She remains one of the most successful African American entertainers of all time.

"You know, friends, that I do not lie to you when I tell you I have walked into the palaces of kings and queens and into the houses of presidents. And much more. But I could not walk into a hotel in America and get a cup of coffee, and that made me mad."

EXPLORE MORE!

Look for the award-winning, beautifully illustrated book *Josephine: The Dazzling Life of Josephine Baker* by Patricia Hruby Powell at your local library.

THURGOOD MARSHALL

1908–1993

Thurgood Marshall was an American lawyer who is credited with winning the landmark case *Brown v. Board of Education*. He was also the first African American Supreme Court Justice.

Thurgood Marshall was born in 1908 in Maryland. His mother was a teacher, and his father was a railroad porter. His parents often took him to see court cases, and the family would talk—and argue—about the cases at home later. Unsurprisingly, Thurgood became a stand-out member of debate teams in school.

After graduating from Lincoln University, Thurgood enrolled at Howard University School of Law. And that's where he found his true calling. He trained under law professors who taught him how to use his natural debate skills and analytical mind to create powerful arguments and support them with evidence. Thurgood especially admired the dean of the law school, Charles Hamilton Houston. Houston spent most of his career attacking segregation laws. He was a difficult and demanding professor, but he taught Thurgood that everyone deserves civil rights, including African Americans.

After graduating, Thurgood briefly had a private law practice, then began working with the National Association for the Advancement of Colored People (NAACP). He argued and won many cases that struck blows to racism. In 1954, he took on what turned out to be his defining achievement: *Brown v. Board of Education of Topeka.* The case centered on Oliver Brown, who filed the lawsuit after his daughter wasn't allowed to enroll in a whites-only public school. Thurgood argued that segregated schools were unconstitutional, and the Supreme Court justices unanimously ruled in his favor. This verdict overturned an earlier court decision that claimed that segregation was legal as long as the schools were "separate but equal." *Brown v. Board of Education* forced all public schools to become integrated.

Thurgood became one of the most successful lawyers in the country. In 1967, he was nominated to serve on the Supreme Court, and he became the first African American Supreme Court justice. He remained on the bench for 24 years.

"Equal means getting the same thing at the same time in the same place."

EXPLORE MORE!

Go to the US Supreme Court website to learn more about the highest court in the land: supremecourt history.org.

DOROTHY HEIGHT

1912–2010

Dorothy Height was an activist, philanthropist, and organizational leader. She was the president of the National Council of Negro Women for 40 years.

Dorothy Height was born in 1912 in Virginia. She became an activist while she was still a teenager, organizing protests against lynchings in the South. Dorothy was a talented orator, or speaker, which she proved by winning a national oratory competition and being awarded with a college scholarship.

Dorothy was admitted to Barnard College in New York in 1929, but before the school year started she was told that the college had already filled its quota of black students and wouldn't admit any more. Dorothy switched her sights to New York University, where she earned a bachelor's degree in education and a master's in psychology.

In 1937, Dorothy joined the Harlem Young Women's Christian Association (YWCA). Dorothy quickly became a leader in the

YWCA and encouraged them to integrate their centers all over the country. She also started their Center for Racial Justice. In 1957, she became president of the National Council of Negro Women (NCNW). She remained as president until 1997, working toward the goals of stopping lynchings of African Americans and reforming the criminal justice system, which favored white people.

Dorothy became a key figure in the civil rights movement and was regularly called on to give advice on political issues. She helped organize the March on Washington, a huge protest march at which Martin Luther King Jr. gave his famous "I Have a Dream" speech. Dorothy was happy to have played a role in the march but troubled that she had not been asked to speak, despite her exceptional skills. She called it "an eye-opening experience."

Dorothy continued to be active in the fight for women's rights as well. She helped found the National Women's Political Caucus with feminist leaders Gloria Steinem, Betty Friedan, and Shirley Chisholm.

Dorothy received the Presidential Medal of Freedom and the Congressional Gold Medal, among many other awards. President Barack Obama called her "the godmother of the civil rights movement and a hero to so many Americans."

"I want to be remembered as someone who used herself and anything she could touch to work for justice and freedom...I want to be remembered as one who tried."

EXPLORE MORE!

The Young Women's Christian Association and National Council of Negro Women are still active organizations. Visit their websites to read what they're doing today.

JESSE OWENS

1913–1980

Jesse Owens was an Olympic track and field athlete. He won four gold medals in the 1936 Olympic Games in Berlin.

Jesse Owens was born James Cleveland Owens in 1913 in Alabama. He was the youngest of 10 children, and had to work hard to help his family by picking cotton. His family moved to Cleveland, Ohio, when Jesse was nine. His thick Southern accent led to the nickname that stayed with him for the rest of his life. When he told a teacher to call him J.C., the teacher thought that he had said "Jesse."

Jesse fell in love with running when he was in junior high. His coach encouraged him to practice whenever he could. By the time he got to high school, he was already gaining national attention for his extraordinary speed in the 100- and 200-yard dashes.

Jesse went to Ohio State University after high school, where he continued to dominate in track and field. Although he was the best on the team, he had to live off campus with other African American athletes. He also had to work part-time jobs in order to pay his tuition, but his busy work and school schedule did not slow him down. Jesse set many track and field records, and people all over the country couldn't wait to see him in the Olympics.

That day came in 1936, when Jesse competed in the Summer Olympics in Berlin, Germany. Adolf Hitler, who led the Nazi party, was in power in Germany at the time. Hitler planned to use the Olympic games to show the world that his belief in the superiority of white people was correct. He expected that Germany would win all of the gold medals. He was wrong. Jesse easily won the 100-dash and the long jump. By the time the Olympics ended, he had won four gold medals, leaving Hitler upset and embarrassed. The United States won a total of 24 gold medals that year.

It took five decades for anyone to match Jesse's record of four gold medals at a single Olympics. He remains one of the most famous track and field athletes of all time.

" We all have dreams. But in order to make dreams come into reality, it takes an awful lot of determination, dedication, self-discipline, and effort."

EXPLORE MORE!

Look for videos of Jesse Owens's record-breaking runs on YouTube.

ROSA PARKS

1913–2005

Rosa Parks was a political activist who became famous for her role in the Montgomery Bus Boycott. She has been called "the mother of the freedom movement" and "the first lady of civil rights."

Rosa Parks was born Rosa Louise McCauley in 1913 in Alabama. When Rosa was two, her mother moved the family to a small farming community called Pine Level to live with Rosa's grandparents. Rosa's grandfather was very outspoken and pushed back against laws that said black people and white people weren't equal. Rosa was inspired by his example and grew up unwilling to bend to oppression.

When Rosa was 11, she moved to Montgomery to attend the Industrial School for Girls. In Montgomery, Rosa saw the unfairness of segregation up close. She later enrolled at Alabama State Teachers College for Negroes, but had to drop out when her grandmother became ill.

At the age of 19, Rosa married a local barber named Raymond Parks. Together they worked with many social justice organizations. Rosa was elected secretary of the Montgomery chapter of the National Association for the Advancement of Colored People (NAACP). Working with the NAACP could be dangerous because members were sometimes harassed or threatened, but Rosa was determined to keep fighting.

Rosa is best known for her role in the Montgomery Bus Boycott. On December 1, 1955, she boarded a bus in Montgomery. She sat in a seat in the middle section of the bus, where black people were allowed to sit but only if no white people were standing. One white passenger didn't have a seat. Since black people and white people weren't allowed to sit in the same row, that meant all the black people in the row had to stand up. Rosa refused and was arrested. After that day, black people in Montgomery refused to ride the bus until the law was changed. The boycott lasted for 381 days.

Many have tried to downplay Rosa's role in the boycott by saying she was just tired that day, but that wasn't true. As she said, "No, the only tired I was, was tired of giving in." Though her role in the boycott is what she is most remembered for, Rosa never stopped fighting for civil rights.

"I would like to be remembered as a person who wanted to be free ... so other people would be also free."

EXPLORE MORE!

Check out a virtual tour of the Rosa Parks Museum on YouTube.

DAISY BATES

1914–1999

Daisy Bates was a civil rights activist and newspaper publisher. Her news reporting documented the battle to end segregation in Arkansas.

Daisy Bates was born in Arkansas in 1914. A horrific tragedy marred her childhood. Daisy's mother was murdered by a group of white men when Daisy was still a little girl. This experience doubtlessly set her on her path to fight against racial violence.

Daisy married young, and she and her husband started their own newspaper, the *Arkansas State Press*. It was one of the only African American newspapers to focus solely on civil rights and the achievements of black people. Daisy became active in the civil rights movement. For many years, she served as the president of the Arkansas chapter of the National Association for the Advancement of Colored People (NAACP).

Daisy's pivotal role in the civil rights movement was sparked by a famous court case. In 1954, the Supreme Court ruled that segregated schools were unconstitutional in *Brown v. Board of Education*. This meant that it was illegal to prevent black children from going to school with white children. But that didn't mean the change came fast or easy. Some white people were angered by the decision and wanted to keep black children out of schools.

A group of nine black children, later known as the Little Rock Nine, enrolled at a high school that had previously been all white. But when they tried to go into the school, a group of white men jeered at them, and the Arkansas governor, who opposed desegregation, sent soldiers to stop the children from entering the building. President Dwight D. Eisenhower later sent troops to protect the children as they entered the school. Daisy supported and advocated for the Little Rock Nine, even though she was harassed and bullied for it. She wrote about the experience in her memoir, *The Long Shadow of Little Rock: A Memoir*, which won the National Book Award.

Daisy's bravery and selflessness made her a key figure in the civil rights movement.

"No man or woman who tries to pursue an ideal in his or her own way is without enemies."

EXPLORE MORE!

Look for *March Forward, Girl: From Young Warrior to Little Rock Nine* by Melba Pattillo Beals to read more about the experiences of the Little Rock Nine.

KATHERINE JOHNSON

1918–2020

K atherine Johnson was a mathematician who worked for NASA. Her calculations were critical to the success of the first crewed space flights.

Katherine Johnson was born Katherine Coleman in 1918 in West Virginia. From an early age, she was gifted in math and science. She whizzed through school and completed eighth grade when she was only 10. The public school for black children in Katherine's community didn't go past eighth grade, so Katherine's parents sent her to a high school on the campus of West Virginia State College. She graduated high school at 14 and went on to attend West Virginia State University. She graduated magna cum laude with degrees in mathematics and French.

Katherine later took a job as a mathematician at the National Advisory Committee for Aeronautics (NACA). She was part of a segregated team of African American women who worked as "human computers," checking male engineers' calculations for flight tests. Katherine and her team members were not allowed to eat with or use the same breakrooms or restrooms as their white colleagues.

Katherine was soon promoted to another department, where she worked with white men. Many tried to discriminate against her, but she stood up for herself and her work. In 1958, NACA became the National Aeronautics and Space Administration (NASA). Katherine was part of a team doing calculations that would help send people into space. Her skills not only made the early space missions successful, but many times she was responsible for plotting the landing of space shuttles, keeping astronauts safe when they returned to Earth.

NASA officials relied on Katherine's accuracy. She was essential to Apollo 11, the United States' first mission to the moon. Though NASA had started to use electronic computers, they still wanted Katherine to check the calculations. Astronaut John Glenn insisted on it!

After a long, successful career at NASA, Katherine retired in 1986. Throughout her career, she dedicated her life to promoting science and mathematics to people of color. She has been recognized with several awards, including a Congressional Gold Medal, and in 2016, NASA formally renamed a research center in her name.

> " Some things will drop out of the public eye and will go away, but there will always be science, engineering, and technology. And there will always, always be mathematics."

EXPLORE MORE!

Do you want to know more about Katherine Johnson and what her years at NASA were like? Watch the 2016 film *Hidden Figures*, or read *Hidden Figures: Young Readers' Edition* by Margot Lee Shetterly.

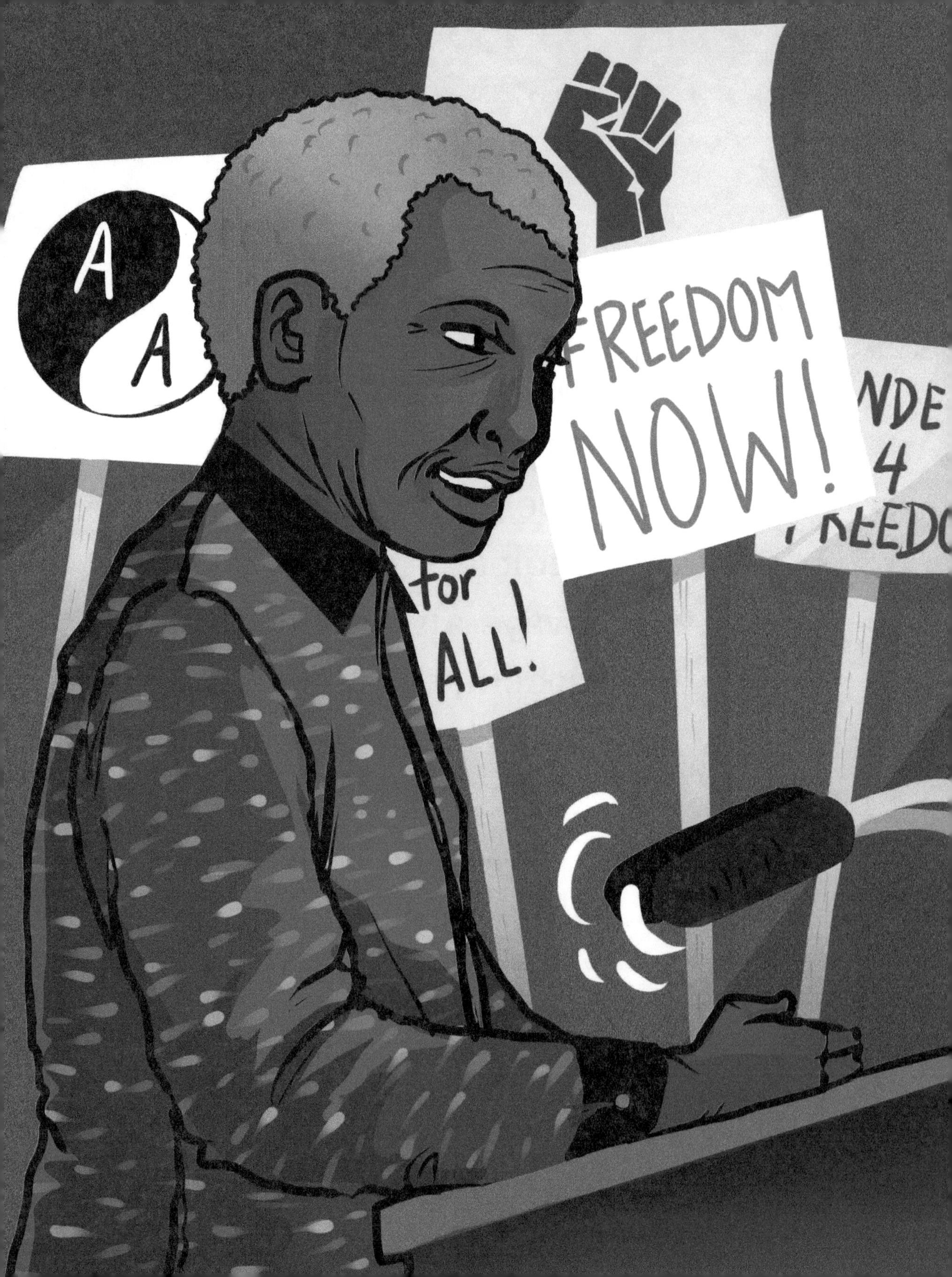
A A
FREEDOM NOW!
for ALL!

NELSON MANDELA

1918–2013

Nelson Mandela was a political leader, anti-apartheid revolutionary, and former president of South Africa. He was his country's first black head of state.

Nelson Mandela was born Rolihlahla Mandela in the village of Mvezo in South Africa in 1918. He was the first person in his family to attend school. His primary school teacher gave him the name Nelson, as it was the custom at the time for teachers to give children "Christian" names. When Nelson was nine years old, his father passed away and Nelson became the ward of the acting leader of the Thembu tribe. Nelson moved from his small village to the chief's royal residence, which gave him the opportunity to continue his education.

At the time, South Africa was racially segregated, with white people holding all of the political and economic power. As a young man, Nelson witnessed how the government put more and more restrictions on the black majority. Nelson soon became involved in anti-apartheid, a political movement that wanted to free black South Africans from oppression. He joined the African National Congress, an organization that fought for black people's rights. He organized and participated in many protests. In 1963, Nelson was arrested and given a life sentence in prison for trying to overthrow the government. He spent 27 years behind bars. While he was in prison, black people in South Africa continued to support him and his cause.

Nelson was released from prison in 1990, and he was elected the president of the African National Congress (ANC) a year later. He led the ANC in negotiations with the government to end apartheid. South Africa's president, F. W. de Klerk, also wanted to end whites-only rule. He and Nelson worked together to bring democracy to South Africa. In 1993, they jointly won the Nobel Peace Prize.

In 1994, South Africa held its first democratic presidential election. Nelson won the election and was president until 1999. But his work was not finished. He continued to fight for democracy and equality for all South Africans. Nelson was a person of principle and integrity and never resorted to violence or answered racism with racism. He has been an inspiration to all who are oppressed or discriminated against.

"I learned that courage was not the absence of fear, but the triumph over it."

EXPLORE MORE!

Check out *Long Walk to Freedom: The Autobiography of Nelson Mandela* to hear about Nelson's life in his own words.

JACKIE ROBINSON

1919–1972

Jackie Robinson was the first African American player in Major League Baseball. His use of nonviolence as a means for change opened the door for others and set an example for the civil rights movement.

Jack Roosevelt Robinson was born in 1919 in Georgia. He was a gifted athlete and played four sports in high school: football, basketball, track, and baseball. He took his talents to UCLA and became the first athlete to win varsity letters in four sports. Unfortunately, he had to drop out of school when it became too difficult financially.

Jackie was drafted into the United States Army, where he was a second lieutenant. During this time, he was arrested when he refused to move to the back of a segregated bus. Jackie was well known and liked, so, with the help of black newspapers and the National Association for the Advancement of Colored People (NAACP), the painful experience drew attention to racial injustice.

In 1945, Jackie joined a baseball team called the Kansas Monarchs, which was one of the Negro Leagues teams. He was extremely popular in the Negro League and soon attracted attention from the Major Leagues. At the time, Major League Baseball didn't allow black players. In 1946, Jackie joined a minor league team called the Montreal Royals.

Jackie did not have an easy time on the team. He faced hostility both on and off the field. Many players refused to play with him, and people in the stands would boo and shout racist terms. Jackie handled the taunting calmly, had an outstanding first season, and was able to join the Major League team the Brooklyn Dodgers. This made him the first black athlete in Major League Baseball, which has been referred to as "breaking the color barrier."

Jackie continued to face racism, with opposing teams and even some of his own teammates threatening not to play with him, but he stayed strong and continued to show his talent. He was selected as the Most Valuable Player of the year in 1949, and in 1955 he helped the Dodgers win the World Series.

Today, Jackie is recognized as one of the most important athletes of the 20th century. Every Major League team honors him on April 15, Jackie Robinson Day.

> **"I'm not concerned with your liking or disliking me.... All I ask is that you respect me as a human being."**

EXPLORE MORE!

Would you like to learn more about baseball and its stand-out players? Read *Baseball Biographies for Kids: The Greatest Players from the 1960s to Today* by Dean Burrell.

MILES DAVIS

1926–1991

Miles Davis was a jazz trumpeter, bandleader, and composer. He is considered to be one of the greatest pioneers in jazz.

Miles Davis was born in 1926 in Illinois. His father was a dentist, and his mother was a music teacher. As a child, Miles was always surrounded by music. When Miles was a teenager, his father gave him a trumpet as a gift. He began taking lessons and quickly fell in love with the instrument. Miles's teacher told him to play without vibrato, which is a pulsating tone used by other trumpeters, like Louis Armstrong. This advice influenced the unique sound Miles became known for.

Miles often entered music competitions in high school, but no matter how well he played, his white classmates were given first place. He said those experiences pushed him to be a better musician. Miles later attended the world-famous Juilliard School of Music (then called the Institute of Musical Art) in New York City. He was enchanted by the local music scene. He played gigs with musicians he admired, like Charlie Parker, in Harlem nightclubs. After three years, Miles dropped out of school to be a full-time jazz musician.

This began a time of exceptional growth in Miles's music. He played in bands and recorded music with Charlie Parker for a few years, all the time experimenting with his own style. He was always looking for something new—a new sound, a new technique, a new way to play the trumpet. He improvised while he played and became known for his original, unexpected performances. Miles struck out on his own and started a nine-piece band that included a French horn, tuba, and baritone saxophone. Songs recorded with that band were later released as an album called *Birth of the Cool*. This album springboarded a new style of music called cool jazz.

Miles's personality, creativity, and talent placed him among the greatest jazz musicians in the 20th century. Throughout his career, he received many awards, including several Grammy Awards for the best jazz performance. Today, Miles is recognized as one of the most influential musicians of all time.

> "Sometimes you have to play a long time to be able to play like yourself."

EXPLORE MORE!

Read *Birth of the Cool: How Jazz Great Miles Davis Found His Sound* by Kathleen Cornell Berman to enjoy the story of Miles Davis in poetic language. You can also find audio recordings of Miles playing his music online.

MARTIN LUTHER KING JR.

1929–1968

Martin Luther King Jr. was a civil rights leader and political activist. The most well-known leader in the civil rights movement, Martin advocated for nonviolence and civil disobedience.

Martin Luther King Jr. was born in 1929 in Georgia. He was the son of a preacher and often watched his father's sermons. Martin's father saw racism as "an affront to God" and instilled this belief in his children. But growing up in the South, Martin often witnessed and experienced acts of racism. This imprinted on his memory, and he vowed to fight against injustice for the rest of his life.

Martin went to Morehouse College, where he was student body president and graduated as valedictorian. By the age of 25, he had a PhD from Boston University and had become a pastor at a Baptist church in Montgomery, Alabama.

Martin became a leading member of the National Association for the Advancement of Colored People (NAACP). He organized nonviolent demonstrations, such as sit-ins, to protest segregation. In 1955, Rosa Parks refused to give up her seat on the bus to a white passenger. The NAACP decided to use this event to fight segregation laws and chose Martin to lead a protest called the Montgomery Bus Boycott. Black people refused to ride the bus until public transportation was desegregated. The boycott lasted for 381 days.

Martin was a skillful speaker who inspired and motivated people with his words. In 1963, he organized the March on Washington along with other African American leaders. This was a huge protest march involving 250,000 people. It became the setting of Martin's famous "I Have a Dream" speech, which called out the injustices faced by African Americans.

In 1964, Martin was awarded with a Nobel Peace Prize for his activism and leadership. Martin fought for civil rights and equality throughout his life, organizing and participating in many other historic protests, such as the Selma to Montgomery March. And though he faced intense danger—his home was even bombed—he never backed down. Tragically, he was assassinated in 1968, but his legacy can't be overstated. He is a national icon for peaceful protest and one of the most influential people from the civil rights movement.

"If you can't fly, then run.
If you can't run, then walk.
If you can't walk, then crawl,
but by all means,
keep moving."

EXPLORE MORE!

Check out civil rights hero John Lewis's book *March: Book One*, the first in a trilogy of graphic novels about Martin Luther King Jr.'s life and role in the civil rights movement.

BARBARA JORDAN

1936–1996

Barbara Jordan was a groundbreaking politician, activist, and educator. She was the first African American elected to Congress from the Deep South.

Barbara Jordan was born in 1936 in Texas. Her father was a preacher, and both of her parents were active leaders in the church. Barbara's parents valued education and encouraged her to work hard in school. She was on her high school's debate team and distinguished herself as a talented speaker who could cleverly argue her positions. She graduated with honors as valedictorian of her class.

Barbara majored in political science and history at Texas Southern University, where she continued to shine in debate. After graduating, she enrolled at Boston University School of Law. She was one of the only black students in her program.

Barbara returned to Texas to begin her law career, but soon she set her sights on entering politics. In 1966, she ran for the Texas senate and won. She became the first black state senator since 1883 and the first black woman ever elected to the Texas senate. As senator, Barbara focused on improving the lives of people struggling in her community. She helped establish a minimum wage to help people living in poverty. Six years later, she was elected to the US House of Representatives as the first woman to represent Texas in Congress.

During Barbara's time as a congresswoman, the country was divided over President Richard Nixon's impeachment trial. In 1974, she made a speech to the judiciary committee. In her speech, which was shown on television throughout the country, she masterfully laid out President Nixon's abuses. Barbara was praised as a distinguished speaker, and people around the world started paying attention. She also used her time in Congress to support bills that opposed discrimination and inequality. Today she is recognized as a trailblazer who broke down barriers for other African Americans in politics.

"My faith in the Constitution is whole; it is complete; it is total. And I am not going to sit here and be an idle spectator to the diminution, the subversion, the destruction of the Constitution . . . It is reason and not passion which must guide our debate and guide our decision."

EXPLORE MORE!

You can watch a video of Barbara Jordan's ground-breaking speech on the impeachment of Richard Nixon on YouTube.

WILMA RUDOLPH

1940–1994

Wilma Rudolph was an Olympic track and field star, and the first American woman to win three gold medals in track and field in a single Olympics.

Wilma Rudolph was born in 1940 in Tennessee. She became one of the fastest runners in the world, but her journey was not easy. When Wilma was five, she was diagnosed with a disease called polio. Many doctors told her that she would need a leg brace to help her walk for her whole life. But Wilma and her parents were hopeful that someday she would be able to walk without help. They sought out the best doctors they could find, but because Wilma grew up in the segregated South, where African Americans were denied access to good medical care, her family had to travel nearly 50 miles to see her doctors. Through great determination, Wilma was walking without a brace by the time she was 12. Within a year she could run faster than any other child in her grade.

In high school, Wilma was an excellent basketball player, but she loved track and field even more. Though she was only 16, Wilma's coaches encouraged her to race in the 1956 Olympic trials. She won a spot on the US Olympic team! At her first Olympics, as the youngest member of her team, Wilma won a bronze medal in the relays.

Wilma competed in her second Olympics in Rome in 1960. In Rome, she set a new record in the 100-meter dash and became the first American woman to win three gold medals in track and field in one Olympics. After the games, people called Wilma the "fastest woman in history." She became famous all around the world as people heard about her amazing accomplishments.

Wilma was not only a superstar athlete. During the civil rights movement, she joined protests and sit-ins, using her popularity to bring attention to racial discrimination. She refused to participate in events that were segregated, including the parade her town threw to celebrate her Olympic victory. Wilma's homecoming parade and banquet were the first integrated events in her town's history.

In 1981, Wilma started the Wilma Rudolph Foundation to support young athletes. She was added to the National Women's Hall of Fame in 1994.

"My doctor told me I would never walk again. My mother told me I would. I believed my mother."

EXPLORE MORE!

Look at clips and images of Wilma Rudolph's stellar career at olympic.org/wilma-rudolph.

MUHAMMAD ALI

1942–2016

Muhammad Ali was a champion boxer and prominent activist. He was one of the most celebrated,
and colorful, sports figures of the 20th century.

Muhammad Ali was born Cassius Marcellus Clay Jr. in 1942 in
Kentucky. As a child, Cassius experienced a lot of discrimination,
and he discovered that boxing was an exciting and constructive
way to release his anger. He started training as a boxer when
he was 12 years old. Though he was young, Cassius soon won
championships in his home state of Kentucky and nationally.
When he was 18, he won a gold medal in the 1960 Olympics
in Rome.

After the Olympics, Cassius began working as a professional
boxer, where he faced much tougher opponents but continued
to show his skill. Cassius not only physically defeated other box-
ers, but he also used his boisterous personality to play with his
opponents' minds. Some commentators and fans believed that
Cassius was boastful, but this tactic worked to his advantage

and made him a beloved public figure. In 1963, though he was the underdog, Cassius shocked the sports world by becoming the youngest heavyweight champion ever. During this time, he converted to Islam and changed his name from Cassius Clay to Muhammad Ali.

In 1966, Muhammad was drafted into the US Army to fight in the Vietnam War. He refused to join, because the war was against the teachings of his Muslim faith. Although it was his right to object to the war because of his religion, Muhammad was arrested for his refusal. He was stripped of his heavyweight champion's title and barred from the sport of boxing. His unjust conviction was eventually overturned by the Supreme Court, and he regained the heavyweight title in 1974.

Throughout his career, Muhammad spoke up against racial injustice and inequality. He donated to charities in the US and around the world. Today, he is considered one of the most influential athletes of all time.

> 66 I am America. I am the part you won't recognize. But get used to me—black, confident, cocky; my name, not yours; my goals, my own. Get used to me."

EXPLORE MORE!

Visit alicenter.org to learn about Muhammad Ali's charity work, efforts to promote peace, and many national and international awards.

✳ MAE JEMISON ✳

1956–

Mae Jemison is an astronaut, physician, and engineer. She was the first black woman to travel to space.

Mae Jemison was born in 1956 in Alabama. She has been fascinated by science since she was a young girl. Mae was a curious and ambitious child. She especially loved studying the human body. Mae's interest in science motivated her to work very hard in school. She graduated from high school early and started college at Stanford University when she was only 16 years old.

As a young college student, Mae faced discrimination because of her race, gender, and age. But Mae was brave and determined. She continued her education at Cornell University, where she earned her medical degree. Mae joined the Peace Corps, where she worked as a doctor in Africa. One of Mae's biggest goals was to use her knowledge to educate others. She wrote manuals to teach people how to take care of their own health, and she helped create guidelines for health and safety issues.

Mae also had dreams of becoming an astronaut. She applied to NASA in 1987. She and just 14 others were selected out of 2,000 applicants. After a year of strenuous training, Mae became the first female African American astronaut! On September 12, 1992, Mae's dreams of going to space came true when she launched in the space shuttle *Endeavour* with six other astronauts. As a scientist on the shuttle, it was Mae's job to run more than 40 scientific experiments, including cell research. Mae spent 190 hours, 30 minutes, and 23 seconds in space. She orbited the Earth 126 times.

After returning to Earth, Mae retired from NASA and founded two technology companies. Mae continues to educate others as a professor to spread her love for science and medicine. Mae is also an important social advocate, working to support more diversity in the sciences and math. In honor of her many amazing accomplishments, Mae was inducted into the International Space Hall of Fame and the National Women's Hall of Fame.

"Being first gives you a responsibility—you have a public platform, and you must choose how to use it. I use mine to help folks become more comfortable with the idea that science is integral to our world. And I vowed that I would talk about my work and ask other women about theirs— the nitty-gritty details."

EXPLORE MORE!

Read *Little Leaders: Bold Women in Black History* by Vashti Harrison to learn more about Mae Jemison and other extraordinary women.

BARACK OBAMA

1961–

Barack Obama is a groundbreaking politician, a lawyer, and the 44th president of the United States. He was the first African American president.

Barack Obama was born in 1961 in Hawaii to an American mother and Kenyan father. Barack was an excellent student throughout his childhood in Hawaii, and he even spent some time living with his family abroad. Barack had big goals after he graduated high school. He decided to attend Occidental College in Los Angeles before transferring to Columbia University in New York City. But he wasn't done studying yet!

After Columbia, Barack went to law school at Harvard, where he became the first African American to lead the *Harvard Law Review*. Once he finished law school, Barack moved to Chicago, where he worked to support local communities. In 1996, Barack began his career in politics to continue helping the communities he loved. He served three terms in the Illinois state senate before becoming a United States senator in 2005. Then, in 2008,

Barack Obama was elected as the 44th president, and the first African American president, of the United States.

After he took office, Barack faced many challenges. His biggest challenge was the Great Recession (2007–2009), a time of extreme financial trouble and high unemployment for the country. During this time, Americans relied on Barack's leadership to guide them through a stock market crash and uncertain futures for many industries and banks. Barack also worked hard to advance international diplomacy while he was president. In 2009, he was awarded a Nobel Peace Prize for his diplomatic efforts.

Throughout his political career, Barack Obama encountered intense racism, but he did not let it slow him down. His presidency demonstrated a big change in race relations. All around the world, people reacted to his success with hope and excitement. At home in the US, many people were—and still are today—inspired by the election of an African American president.

"Keep exploring. Keep dreaming. Keep asking why. Don't settle for what you already know. Never stop believing in the power of your ideas, your imagination, your hard work to change the world."

EXPLORE MORE!

Check out Barack Obama's children's book, *Of Thee I Sing: A Letter to My Daughters*, to hear his perspective in his own words.

VENUS WILLIAMS

1980–

SERENA WILLIAMS

1981–

Venus and Serena Williams are sisters and champion tennis players. Combined, over 17 years, they won 12 Wimbledon singles titles, one of the biggest titles in tennis.

Venus and Serena Williams were raised by their father in California. They began playing tennis together when they were only three years old. Their father pushed them to work hard at the sport and they would play hours a day, day after day. They played on run-down courts with tattered nets in a poor area of Compton, California. When Venus was only 10, her tennis serve was almost 100 miles per hour. At 12, she was undefeated in junior tennis, having won 63 matches and lost none.

In 1991, the family moved to Florida so that the girls could attend a tennis academy. For four years, they practiced tennis for six hours a day, six days a week. But despite the emphasis on tennis, Venus and Serena's parents also valued their education. They insisted that their daughters study hard to help guarantee a successful future.

Serena and Venus both started playing professionally as young teenagers. The fans loved them instantly! The sisters are known for being amazingly fast and powerful players. Their strength and speed changed how women's tennis is played.

Venus and Serena sometimes play as a team (called doubles tennis) and sometimes as single players. As single players, they have competed against each other more than 20 times. They have won 14 Grand Slam titles and three Olympic gold medals playing together. Each of them has also won an Olympic gold medal as a single player.

Despite the sisters' success, they have often faced racism and gender discrimination. Players and sports commentators have used racial slurs and insults when they talk about how Serena and Venus look or play. Nonetheless, the sisters do their best to ignore the insults, knowing that they are excellent players. Today, both sisters continue to be ranked among the top athletes in the world.

> " You have to believe in yourself when no one else does—that makes you a winner right there."

—Venus Williams

> " I really think a champion is defined not by their wins but by how they can recover when they fall."

—Serena Williams

EXPLORE MORE!

Research Althea Gibson to get to know a tennis great who inspired the Williams sisters.

MORE INSPIRING PEOPLE TO EXPLORE!

MAYA ANGELOU (1928–2014) was a renowned poet and civil rights activist. She used her writings to give voice to the black community.

ARTHUR ASHE (1943–1993) was a tennis player. Throughout his career, Arthur won countless championships, including three Grand Slam titles.

SHIRLEY CHISHOLM (1924–2005) was a politician and activist. She was the first black woman elected to Congress, and later she became the first woman to run for president.

COUNTEE CULLEN (1903–1946) was a poet and playwright. Countee was one of the most prominent writers during the Harlem Renaissance of the 1920s.

CHARLES R. DREW (1904–1950) was a leading doctor. His research helped advance and promote the use of blood transfusions and blood banks.

FANNIE LOU HAMER (1917–1977) was a civil rights activist and politician. During the 1960s, Fannie worked tirelessly to register African Americans to vote. Her work resulted in the passing of the monumental Voting Rights Act of 1965.

MATTHEW HENSON (1866–1955) was an explorer. He was a part of the first expedition that reached the North Pole.

OSCAR MICHEAUX (1884–1951) was a leading filmmaker and director. He produced nearly 44 films throughout his career.

DORIS "DORIE" MILLER (1919–1943) was a sailor in the Navy. During the 1941 attack on Pearl Harbor, Doris helped shoot down several Japanese planes. He was later recognized by the Navy as a hero in World War II.

GARRETT MORGAN (1877–1963) was an inventor and leader. Garrett is responsible for several modern-day inventions, including the traffic light and smoke hood.

TONI MORRISON (1931–2019) was a renowned writer and educator. In 1988, she won the Pulitzer Prize for her book *Beloved*.

COLIN POWELL (1937–) is a leading politician and one of just a few four-star African American generals. From 2001 to 2005, Colin served as the US secretary of state. He was the first African American to hold this position.

A. PHILIP RANDOLPH (1889–1979) was a leading activist, organizer, and politician. He was a key organizer in the 1963 March on Washington.

MARY CHURCH TERRELL (1863–1954) was an activist and educator. She was one of the first African American women to earn a college degree.

MALCOLM X (1925–1965) was a minister and civil rights activist. Malcolm X was one of the most influential leaders in African American history.

ACKNOWLEDGMENTS

Many thanks to: The History Consultants LLC and Dr. Kimberly Brown Pellum.

ABOUT THE AUTHOR

Arlisha Norwood received her PhD in history from Howard University.

Her research examines the experiences of single African American women in post-Civil War Virginia. In addition to research, she focuses on developing her passion for public history. She has worked for several museums, historic sites, and cultural organizations including the Smithsonian Institution's National Museum for African American History and Culture, and the National Park Service. She is committed to engaging a broader audience and transmitting her love for history through innovative and exciting methods.

NOTES

NOTES

NOTES

NOTES

NOTES

NOTES

NOTES

NOTES

NOTES

NOTES

NOTES